Copyright

D1616262

Table of Contents

Introduction

Christmas is a busy time for most families. You are fresh off all the hard work of Thanksgiving and also making plans for the New Year. You have probably been invited to many parties in between family, work, and friends, and wonder when you will have time to get everything done for your own party. Whether you plan to have a big bash for your family at your home this year or you just want to make some great creations for your spouse and family to enjoy during the holiday season, this is the recipe book for you.

Inside this book, you will find all the great classic Christmas recipes that you grew up with and will want to share with your family. And all of these recipes can be started in a slow cooker in just minutes. Rather than spending a lot of time at the oven, hoping to get it all done in time, you can throw these in a few hours before your party or before dinner, and have everything ready with minimal work. You have enough to worry about during the holidays, why let the cooking stress you out?

From holiday drinks, to side dishes, main courses, and even desserts, take a look through this recipe book to get started on your meal planning for the holidays and be the one to go to for the best cooking next year.

Drinks to Warm You Inside and Out

Chocolate Peppermint Surprise

Holiday Rum

The holidays are not complete without something fun for the adults. This is the perfect drink to try out. It allows your guests to have some fun without leaving anyone too tipsy to drive home.

Ingredients:
Ground nutmeg
Whipped cream
2 c. rum
½ tsp. nutmeg
6 whole cloves
3 cinnamon sticks
1 pinch salt
½ c. butter
2 c. brown sugar
6 c. water

Directions:
1. Place all the ingredients, excluding the ground nutmeg, cream, and rum, into a slow cooker.
2. Add the water, cover and cook the drink on a low setting for about 5 hours.
3. Add the rum and stir. Pour the hot drink into mugs and then top with the cream and some nutmeg. Serve warm.

Serves 8
Per Serving
Calories   218
Fat   10 g.
Carbs   15 g.
Protein   1 g.

Chocolate Peppermint Surprise

Chocolate and peppermint are staples in every home during the holidays. And with this tasty and warm drink, you are sure to please everyone.

Ingredients:
7 c. water
1 tsp. peppermint flavoring
½ c. chocolate syrup
¼ tsp. salt
¾ c. cocoa powder
1 c. sugar
3 c. dried milk powder

Directions:
1. Mix all of the dry ingredients together in the slow cooker. Pour in the chocolate syrup and the peppermint and mix well.
2. While whisking the ingredients together, slowly pour in the water until everything is well mixed.
3. Cover and let the drink cook for 3 hours on a high setting.
4. Serve with a Gingerbread Man dipped in if desired.

Serves 10
Per Serving
Calories   118
Fat   11 g.
Carbs   8 g.
Protein   0 g.

Cherry Cider

While most families like to go with apple cider, a cherry cider can make things even better. Give this a try to get something new during the holidays.

Ingredients:
2 packs cherry gelatin
2 cinnamon sticks
3 ½ qts. Apple cider

Directions:
1. Pour the cider into the slow cooker and add the cinnamon sticks. Cook on a high setting for about 3 hours.
2. After three hours, add in the gelatin and continue cooking for another hour to let the gelatin dissolve.

Serves 12
Per Serving
Calories	211
Fat	5 g.
Carbs	23 g.
Protein	1 g.

Cranberry Punch

Whether you are serving to adults, children, or both of them combined, this is the perfect option. It has all of the fruity goodness that you want while also quenching any thirst you get from the meal.

Ingredients:
1 cinnamon stick
1 tsp. whole cloves
1 c. water
½ c. brown sugar
4 c. cranberry juice
4 c. pineapple juice

Directions:
1. Wrap the cinnamon and cloves up in a piece of cheesecloth.
2. Place the cheesecloth inside the slow cooker and add the rest of the ingredients.
3. Cook the mixture for about 4 hours on a low setting. Keep the heat on low for serving.

Serves 12
Per Serving
Calories	187
Fat	6 g.
Carbs	22 g.
Protein	1 g.

Spiced Tea

Having a nice cup of tea during the holidays can really warm you up and help you to feel amazing. With this spiced version, you will really be feeling the holiday cheer.

Ingredients:
2 Tbsp. lemon juice
3 Tbsp. honey
1 c. passion fruit juice
1 cinnamon stick
4 star anise
3 tea bags
2 c. water

Directions:
1. Add in the cinnamon, anise, and tea bags to boiling water. Reducing the heat.
2. Simmer the mixture for about 5 minutes. After 5 minutes, remove the cinnamon and tea bags then add the lemon juice, honey, and nectar.
3. Pour into four cups and enjoy.

Serves 4
Per Serving
Calories   210
Fat   5 g.
Carbs   23 g.
Protein   5 g.

Apple Sparkler

This sparkler just takes a few minutes to make but is sure to be a huge hit will all of your guests when they feel thirsty. Get ready to share this recipe with everyone on your list.

Ingredients:
1 bottle sparkling apple cider
2/3 c. raspberry juice
5 wooden skewers
4 unpeeled lime wedges
10 unpeeled orange wedges
1 Tbsp. colored green sugar

Directions:
1. Sprinkle the colored sugar onto some wax paper. Moisten the tips of your wine glasses and then dip into the sugar. Set these to the side to dry.
2. Place 1 lime and 2 orange wedges onto each skewer.
3. Divide up the raspberry juice between the wine glasses, place the skewers inside the glasses and serve.

Serves 5
Per Serving
Calories   188
Fat   4 g.
Carbs   18 g.
Protein   2 g.

White Hot Chocolate

No holiday is complete without plenty of hot chocolate. But if you're tired of your traditional hot chocolate, give this recipe a try!

Ingredients:
¼ tsp. almond flavoring
1 tsp. vanilla
1/8 tsp. nutmeg
Cinnamon
¾ c. vanilla baking pieces
3 c. light cream

Directions:
1. Combine ¼ cup of the light cream with the vanilla candy, the nutmeg, and the cinnamon, in a pan. Heat on a low heat and whisk to get the vanilla candy to melt.
2. Add the rest of the cream and whisk to combine. Take off the heat before adding the almond and the vanilla. Serve warm.

Serves 5
Per Serving

Calories	274
Fat	12 g.
Carbs	19 g.
Protein	1 g.

Champaign Punch

A nice drink for the adults can be a great touch when you are looking to please everyone. With this option, you can't go wrong. No, you don't use a crockpot but it's a great drink to serve your guests.

Ingredients:
1 kiwi fruit, peeled and sliced
4 strawberries, sliced
16 sugar cubes
¼ c. lemon juice
750 ml. chilled champagne
750 ml. chilled dry white wine
1 can pineapple chunks

Directions:
1. Drain the pineapple saving the juice in a bowl. Stir in the lemon juice, champagne, and wine together in the same bowl..
2. Place one sugar cube in every glass and pour the punch on top.
3. Serve this with skewers of the pineapple, kiwi fruit, and strawberries.

Serves 16
Per Serving
Calories   219
Fat   6 g.
Carbs   21 g.
Protein   0 g.

Spiced Cappuccino

Coffee lovers can enjoy this great holiday as well. With the spiced cappuccino, you will soon hope that Christmas will last all year.

Ingredients:
½ c. vanilla ice cream
Cinnamon
¼ c. liquid nondairy creamer
1 c. hot espresso
Cardamom if desired

Directions:
1. In a 2 cup measuring cup and stir together the cinnamon, creamer, and hot espresso.
2. Divide the mixture between two cups or mugs.
3. Add in the ice cream to both of your cups and sprinkle on a bit of cardamom if you would like before serving.

Serves 2
Per Serving

Calories	211
Fat	10 g.
Carbs	13 g.
Protein	1 g.

Appetizers and Side Dishes

Mashed Potatoes

Herbed Potatoes

Potatoes are a staple in every household when it comes to the holidays. When you are looking for a great recipe that doesn't take very long to cook, these herbed potatoes are the perfect option.

Ingredients:
2 ½ c. cream
¼ tsp. pepper
1 tsp. salt
1 stick melted butter
½ diced onion
6 potatoes, sliced
¼ c. flour
1 handful walnuts
1 ½ c. gruyere cheese, shredded
1 tsp. sage, dried

Directions:
1. Whisk together the cream and the butter. Once smooth, add the spices.
2. Slice the potatoes and the onions. Layer them on top of each other inside your slow cooker. Pour the butter and cream mixture on top.
3. Top the whole dish with the walnuts and the gruyere cheese. Place the lid on top and cook the potatoes on a high setting for 4 hours.

Serves 8
Per Serving
Calories	235
Fat	11 g.
Carbs	18 g.
Protein	2 g.

Poultry Stuffing

Don't rely on stuffing from a box this year. With this quick and simple crock pot recipe, you will have the best stuffing ever and it will be homemade.

Ingredients:
½ tsp. marjoram
1 tsp. thyme
1 ½ tsp. sage
1 tsp. poultry seasoning
12 ½ c. dry bread crumbs
12 oz. sliced mushrooms
¼ c. parsley
2 c. chopped celery
2 c. chopped onion
1 c. butter
2 beaten eggs
4 ½ c. chicken broth
½ tsp. pepper
1 ½ tsp. salt

Directions:
1. Melt the butter in a skillet then add in the mushrooms, parsley, celery, and onion. Cook until the onion becomes opaque.
2. Add the breadcrumbs to a large bowl and spoon the vegetables on top. Season this mixture using the pepper, salt, marjoram, thyme, sage, and poultry seasoning and stir well.
3. Pour in the beaten eggs as well as just enough of the broth to make the mixture moist. Place into the slow cooker and cover.
4. Cook on a high setting for 45 minutes. Then cook for about 5 hours on a low setting.

Serves 12
Per Serving
Calories   211

Fat	4 g.
Carbs	21 g.
Protein	4 g.

Little Smokies

Little smokies go well with any meal that you are cooking and will bring your guests back to memories of parties with their families.

Ingredients:
1 jar grape jelly
1 bottle chili sauce
1 lb. little smokies sausage

Directions:
1. Place the smokies in the slow cooker. Cover with the chili sauce and stir in order to blend then add the grape jelly.
2. Cover and cook for 4 hours on a low setting or until the smokies are heated through.
3. Provide toothpicks to serve directly from the slow cooker.

Serves 16
Per Serving

Calories	167
Fat	11 g.
Carbs	4 g.
Protein	22 g.

Corn Pudding

Mix things up a little bit this holiday season with this tasty corn pudding. Cooks in just three hours and makes a great side dish.

Ingredients:
Grated cheese
¼ tsp. pepper
½ tsp. salt
½ c. evaporated milk
4 eggs
1 can creamed corn
¼ c. chopped tomatoes
¼ c. chopped green pepper
¼ c. chopped onion

Directions:
1. Saute the green peppers and onions in some butter until they become soft. Add in the tomatoes and cook for another minute.
2. In a bowl, whisk together the pepper, salt, cream corn, milk, and eggs. Add the vegetables and combine.
3. Grease the slow cooker a bit before adding the mixture. Cook this on a high setting for 3 hours.
4. Right before serving this pudding, add a bit of cheese and cook to help it melt before serving.

Serves 8
Per Serving
Calories   127
Fat   2 g.
Carbs   12 g.
Protein   1 g.

Apple and Sweet Potato Casserole

Sweet potatoes are a staple at the dinner table, but why not switch it up and try out this casserole that combines these two great flavors.

Ingredients:
2 c. mini marshmallows
½ c. brown sugar
½ tsp. cinnamon
1 tsp. vanilla
1 stick melted butter
5 sweet potatoes, chopped and peeled
2 apples, chopped and peeled

Directions:
1. Place the prepared apples and sweet potatoes inside a bowl. In another bowl, mix together the brown sugar, melted butter, and vanilla.
2. Sprinkle some cinnamon over the apples and potatoes before pouring the brown sugar mixture on top.
3. Pour everything into the slow cooker. Cook either on a high setting for 5 hours or a low setting for 8.
4. Right before serving, add the marshmallows to the top and enjoy.

Serves 8
Per Serving
Calories   248
Fat   14 g.
Carbs   22 g.
Protein   1 g.

Bacon and Beans

Simple and easy, this is the recipe that should be on your favorite list no matter what kind of party you are throwing.

Ingredients:
¼ c. ground red pepper
1 tsp. dry mustard
1 ½ tsp. Worcestershire sauce
½ c. molasses
½ c. ketchup
¼ c. packed brown sugar
4 cans pork and beans
1 c. onion
4 bacon slices

Directions:
1. Cook the bacon in a skillet on medium heat. Drain the cooked bacon on paper towels then crumble it up.
2. Place the bacon into the slow cooker along with the rest of the ingredients, making sure to stir well.
3. Place the lid on top and cook this meal for about 4 hours using the low setting before serving.

Serves 12
Per Serving
Calories   119
Fat   5 g.
Carbs   11 g.
Protein   6g.

Three Bean Casserole
Get all the protein that you need out of this three bean casserole. It tastes great and will have people thinking you bought the dish from the store.

Ingredients:
½ c. ketchup
2 Tbsp. mustard
¼ c. brown sugar
1 minced garlic clove
1 chopped onion
1 lb. ground beef
2 c. garbanzo beans
2 c. lima beans
2 c. red beans
Pepper
Salt
¼ c. red wine
1 tsp. cumin powder.

Directions:
1. Pour the garbanzo and lima beans into the slow cooker.
2. Brown the ground beef with the garlic and onions in a skillet.
3. Add the pepper, salt, red wine, cumin powder, ketchup, mustard, and sugar to the skillet. When hot, add the beef mixture to the beans in the slow cooker.
4. Cook this dish for about 4 hours on a low setting.

Serves 8
Per Serving
Calories   218
Fat   8 g.
Carbs   11 g.
Protein   1 g.

Sweet Potatoes

Make it simple this holiday season when you have so many other things to worry about. Sweet potatoes make the perfect side dish that everyone will enjoy.

Ingredients:
2 Tbsp. flour
1/3 c. pecans
½ c. milk
2 beaten eggs
1 Tbsp. orange juice
2 Tbsp. brown sugar
1/3 c. brown sugar
2 Tbsp. sugar
1/3 c. and 2 Tbsp. melted butter
2 cans sweet potatoes

Directions:
1. Mash the sweet potatoes inside a big bowl. Add in 2 Tbsp. of brown sugar, the sugar, and 1/3 c. of butter.
2. In another bowl mix the milk, eggs, and orange juice together. Add to the sweet potatoes.
3. Place everything inside the slow cooker. In another bowl, mix together the rest of the butter, brown sugar, and the pecans. Pour over the sweet potatoes.
4. Cover and cook on a high setting for about 4 hours before serving.

Serves 8
Per Serving
Calories	176
Fat	3 g.
Carbs	19 g.
Protein	3 g.

Honeyed Carrots

You can never have too many vegetables at the dinner table. But with this great recipe, your guests will think they are getting something like a treat rather than something that is really good for them.

Ingredients:
¼ tsp. pepper
¼ tsp. salt
½ tsp. cinnamon
¼ tsp. ginger
1 Tbsp. butter
2 Tbsp. honey
½ c. orange juice
4 c. baby carrots

Directions:
1. Combine tall of the ingredients in the slow cooker.
2. Cover and cook on low for 4 hours or until the carrots are soft. Serve warm.

Serves 12
Per Serving

Calories	217
Fat	7 g.
Carbs	15 g.
Protein	5 g.

A Side of Green Beans

Green bean casseroles are a great addition to fill up your guests and get them ready for the main dish.

Ingredients:
6 oz. chopped pancetta
10 oz. cheesy alfredo sauce
1 c. roasted bell peppers
28 oz. green beans
2 ½ oz. canned French Fried Onions
½ tsp. pepper

Directions:
1. Place all of the ingredients except the French Fried Onions into the slow cooker.
2. Cover and cook on a high setting for about 4 hours or until the green beans are cooked through.
3. With about 20 minutes left before you are done cooking, add in the onions on top and finish cooking. Serve hot.

Serves 9
Per Serving
Calories   177
Fat   2 g.
Carbs   11 g.
Protein   3 g.

Mint Potatoes

Plain old potatoes are so last year. Add a little bit of spice as well as some mint to bring in a more festive flair to this holiday staple.

Ingredients:
4 Tbsp. chopped mint
2 Tbsp. butter
2 Tbsp. lemon juice
1 tsp. grated lemon pee
¼ tsp. pepper
¼ tsp. garlic powder
¾ tsp. dried oregano
1 tsp. salt
3 Tbsp. olive oil
2 lbs. red potatoes

Directions:
1. Evenly cover the potatoes with the pepper, garlic powder, oregano, salt, and the oil. Place into the slow cooker and let this all cook on a low setting for about 7 hours or until the potatoes are soft.
2. Add the butter, half of the mint, and the lemon peel and juice. Cook with these ingredients for 15 more minutes.
3. Right before serving the potatoes, add in the rest of the mint and enjoy.

Serves 10
Per Serving
Calories   217
Fat   13 g.
Carbs   21 g.
Protein   2g.

Grandma's Mashed Potatoes

Grandma will be so proud when you are able to make a recipe that is just like hers. Make sure to make extras as people will come back for seconds.

Ingredients:
6 c. mashed potatoes
Pepper
Salt
1 pkg. ranch dressing mix
1 tsp. dried parsley flakes
¼ c. softened butter
½ c. sour cream
3 oz. cream cheese

Directions:
1. In a bowl, mix together the black pepper, salt, parsley flakes, butter, sour cream, and cream cheese to make them smooth and soft.
2. Add in the mashed potatoes, taking the time to blend well. Place in the slow cooker, adding in a little extra butter as you go.
3. Put the cover on top of the slow cooker. Cook for 4 hours on a low setting before serving.

Serves 12
Per Serving
Calories   243
Fat   11 g.
Carbs   24 g.
Protein   3 g.

Main Dishes

Christmas Turkey

Honey Ham

Ham is a great option to have on Christmas day. Whether this is in addition to turkey or another meat or on its, own, give this a try for your next meal.

Ingredients:
1 tsp. Worcestershire sauce
1 tsp. cinnamon
2 tsp. thyme
1 Tbsp. brown sugar
1 bone-in ham
¼ c. melted butter
¼ c. honey
¼ c. apple cider vinegar

Directions:
1. Place the ham inside the slow cooker.
2. In another bowl, whisk together all of the other ingredients. Pour this mixture on top of the ham.
3. Place the lid on top of the slow cooker and let this cook on a low setting for about 6 hours.
4. Right before serving, use the drippings to glaze the ham.

Serves 12
Per Serving
Calories   313
Fat   23 g.
Carbs   5 g.
Protein   16 g.

Savory Turkey Breasts

Try something different and make a new tradition with these tasty and savory turkey breasts your family is sure to love.

Ingredients:

3 Tbsp. butter
1 pkg. dry Onion soup mix
1 turkey breast, bone-in

Directions:

1. Rub the soup mix on all sides of the turkey.
2. Place the butter on the bottom of the slow cooker and then put your prepared turkey on the top.
3. Cook the turkey for about 7 hours on a low setting.
4. When you are ready to serve, use some of the drippings in the slow cooker as the sauce on the turkey.

Serves 8

Per Serving

Calories	255
Fat	14 g.
Carbs	5 g.
Protein	11 g.

Vegetarian Pot Pie

Christmas brings out all of your family members, even the vegetarians. Rather than worrying about what to serve them, make this pot pie that is perfect for vegetarians as well as all your other guests.

Ingredients:
½ c. melted butter
½ c. flour
1 ¼ c. water
1 diced onion
½ c. peas
1 c. chopped celery
1 c. chopped carrots
2 cubed potatoes
1 c. vegetable broth
2/3 c. milk
2 ¼ c. Bisquick
1 tsp. parsley
1 tsp. thyme
½ tsp. pepper
½ tsp. garlic powder
1 tsp. salt

Directions:
1. Place the onion, peas, celery, carrots, potatoes, and broth inside a large slow cooker.
2. In another bowl combine the parsley, thyme, pepper, garlic powder, salt, butter, flour, and water so they become smooth.
3. Pour this into the slow cooker and then mix everything together so it's combined. Place the lid on top and cook for an hour on a high setting.
4. In another bowl combine the milk and the baking mixture. Spread this out on top of the other mixtures in the slow cooker.
5. Reduce the heat and let this cook for another 2 hours before serving.

Serves 5
Per Serving
Calories   383
Fat   16 g.
Carbs   23 g.
Protein   4 g.

Ham and Cheese Crackers Dinner

Tired of all the normal and boring ham recipes out there? Make this casserole and find out how easy pleasing all your guests can be.

Ingredients:
2/3 c. evaporated milk
2 Tbsp. vegetable oil
2 Tbsp. butter
1 sliced onion
4 sliced potatoes
1/3 c. BBQ sauce
1 egg
½ c. crushed cheese crackers
2 c. ham, ground
Pepper
Paprika
Salt
1 c. mozzarella cheese, grated

Directions:
1. In a bowl mix together the BBQ sauce, egg, cheese crackers, and ham. Shape into patties.
2. Cook the onions and potatoes in a skillet with the vegetable oil and butter, making sure to turn often in order to avoid burning.
3. When these are done cooking, drain them out and put into the slow cooker.
4. In another bowl, mix the paprika, pepper, salt, cheese, and milk together. Pour on top of the potatoes.
5. Layer your ham patties over this mixture. Place the lid on top and let this cook for 5 hours on a low setting before serving.

Serves 8
Per Serving
Calories   401
Fat   19 g.

| Carbs | 22 g. |
| Protein | 8 g. |

Game Hens

Game hens can be an elegant yet simple way to impress your guests. This recipe can be done in the slow cooker to make things even easier for you.

Ingredients:
2 c. BBQ sauce
2 game hens

Directions:
1. Place the BBQ sauce and game hens in a bowl and let them marinate for about 20 minutes on all sides.
2. Place the game hens into the slow cooker and cook on a low setting for about 10 hours.

Serves 2
Per Serving

Calories	218
Fat	7 g.
Carbs	4 g.
Protein	15 g.

Beef Roast Stir Fry

Nothing is better than stir-fry when you need to make a meal for friends or family. This one can be started ahead of time and be done just in time for everyone to enjoy with some sticky rice.

Ingredients:
1 bag onions and peppers
2 tsp. ginger root
2 Tbsp. rice vinegar
2 Tbsp. ketchup
¾ stir fry sauce
½ tsp. pepper
½ tsp. salt
3 lbs. beef roast

Directions:
1. Season the roast with salt and pepper and brown on all sides in a skillet.
2. Add the beef to the slow cooker. You may have to cut the beef in half to fit.
3. In a small bowl, mix together the ginger, rice vinegar, ketchup, and stir fry sauce. Pour this on top of the beef.
4. Place the lid on top of your slow cooker and let the beef cook for 8 hours on low.
5. When there is about 20 minutes left, add the onions and peppers to the slow cooker and increase to a high setting. Serve warm with some nice white sticky rice.

Serves 4
Per Serving
Calories   315
Fat   13 g.
Carbs   11 g.
Protein   18 g.

Christmas Mac and Cheese

Bring out the inner child in all of your guests with this simple mac and cheese recipe.

Ingredients:
2 c. uncooked macaroni
1 ½ c. grated cheese
3 c. milk
½ tsp. paprika
¼ tsp. onion powder
¼ tsp. pepper
1 tsp. salt
¼ c. flour

Directions:
1. Spray the slow cooker with cooking spray to prevent sticking.
2. In a pan, mix together the garlic powder, onion, pepper, salt, and flour.
3. Add in the milk and turn on the heat. Stir so that all the lumps are gone. Allow the mixture to boil in order to thicken.
4. Add in the cheese and stir to make the mixture smooth before adding in the macaroni to heat up.
5. Pour this whole mixture into your slow cooker. Cover and cook on a low setting for 2 hours.

Serves 8
Per Serving
Calories   389
Fat   11 g.
Carbs   24 g.
Protein   5 g.

Christmas Turkey

Go the traditional route with this easy turkey recipe. Add in the extras and some of your favorite sides, and you soon have a meal for the whole family.

Ingredients:
1 c. green beans
½ c. cream
1 Tbsp. parsley, dried
8 oz. sliced mushrooms
1 sliced onion
2 Tbsp. balsamic vinegar
½ c. beef broth
2 lbs. turkey breast

Directions:
1. Add the turkey to the slow cooker and pour the balsamic vinegar and broth on top.
2. Add the parsley, onions, and mushrooms. Let this all cook on a low setting for about six hours.
3. Add in the beans and the cream to the slow cooker. Let this cook on a high setting for another 30 minutes before serving.

Serves 10
Per Serving

Calories	454
Fat	11 g.
Carbs	21 g.
Protein	22 g.

Fruity Roast Pork

Roasted pork is always a good addition to your family meals. But if you really want to make a splash, add some fruit and see how great pork roast can be.

Ingredients:
¼ tsp. cinnamon
½ tsp. nutmeg
½ tsp. salt
½ c. apple juice
1 pack dried pears
2 lb. pork loin roast
1 sliced onion

Directions:
1. Place the pork loin into the slow cooker. Layer the onions and pears on top of the pork roast.
2. In a bowl, whisk the rest of the ingredients until they are smooth. Pour this over the roast.
3. Cook the meal on a low setting for about 8 hours or until the roast is cooked through.
4. Glaze the meat with the drippings in the slow cooker before serving the dish warm.

Serves 10
Per Serving
Calories   312
Fat   8 g.
Carbs   18 g.
Protein   16 g.

Tenderloin Tips

Add a bit of elegance and class and serve your guests a dish they won't soon forget with these great tenderloin tips.

Ingredients:
1 can tomatoes, diced
1 ½ c. sliced onions
1 Tbsp. vegetable oil
¼ tsp. pepper
1 bag green beans
1 tsp. sugar
1 tsp. salt
3 Tbsp. flour
1 ½ lbs. trimmed beef tip steak

Directions:
1. Mix together the seasonings and the flour then rub it all over the beef. Brown the beef a bit on all sides.
2. Layer the onions inside the slow cooker then the tomatoes and the beef. Top it all with the sugar.
3. Place the lid on top and cook this meal on a low setting for about 8 hours or until the steak is completely cooked.
4. A half hour before serving, place the green beans into the slow cooker and continue cooking for another 30 minutes. Serve warm.

Serves 8
Per Serving
Calories   388
Fat   17 g.
Carbs   11 g.
Protein   14 g.

Potatoes and Pot Roast

Go the traditional route and make a great pot roast with potatoes. You can make extras to feed all your guests, even when you are really busy that day.

Ingredients:
1 chopped onion
1 lb. baby potatoes
1 pack onion and mushroom soup mix
½ c. water
2 ½ lbs. beef chuck roast
½ c. steak sauce

Directions:
1. Whisk together the soup mix, water, and steak sauce until well combined.
2. In the slow cooker layer in the meat and the vegetables so they fit well. Place the lid on top and cook the meal on a low setting for about 8 hours. Serve warm.

Serves 12
Per Serving

Calories	498
Fat	20 g.
Carbs	12 g.
Protein	25 g.

Cheesy Chicken Meal

Cheese and chicken go hand and hand when it comes to great holiday recipes. This recipe has extra cheese to keep your guests and family grinning all season long.

Ingredients:
¼ c. chopped parsley
8 skinned chicken thighs
1 Tbsp. Worcestershire sauce
¼ lb. cheddar cheese
1 can chicken soup
1 tsp. paprika
1 chopped green pepper
1 lb. sliced baby potatoes

Directions:
1. Place the peppers in a layer on the bottom of the slow cooker. Add the potatoes on top.
2. Rub the paprika all over the chicken before putting it into the slow cooker and covering with the soup.
3. Cook this dish for about 6 hours on a low setting or until the chicken is cooked through.
4. Add in the Worcestershire sauce and the cheese. Stir to combine. Serve with some parsley on top.

Serves 6
Per Serving
Calories	238
Fat	9 g.
Carbs	13 g.
Protein	17g.

Swiss Steak

Steaks can be an easy addition to your family meals in the winter time. They can bring you back to summer grilling, all while using your slow cooker.

Ingredients:
½ c. grated Swiss cheese
1 chopped green pepper
½ c. beef broth
1 can diced tomatoes
¼ c. tomato paste
¼ c. flour
1 lb. chuck blade beef

Directions:
1. Dredge the steak through the flour. Sear the steak in a skillet so it becomes browned all over.
2. On the bottom of the slow cooker, add in the tomato paste, broth, and the tomatoes in an even layer.
3. Add in the peppers and the meat before placing the lid on top. Cook the meal for about 10 hours on a low setting.
4. Add a bit of cheese on the top of the meal before serving.

Serves 4
Per Serving
Calories   301
Fat   18 g.
Carbs   5 g.
Protein   21 g.

Sausage Meatloaf

Meatloaf is a great addition to your recipe book and with a bit of sausage added in, you have the perfect meal to bring your whole family to the table.

Ingredients:
1 ½ c. cracker crumbs
1 can cream of mushroom soup
1 c. sour cream
½ tsp. pepper
2 tsp. salt
1 chopped garlic clove
2 chopped onions
½ lb. sausage
2 lbs. ground beef.
1 ½ c. milk

Directions:
1. Soak the cracker crumbs with the milk. Add the pepper, salt, garlic, onions, sausage, and beef into the bowl and mix them all together.
2. In another bowl blend together the mushroom soup and the sour cream until smooth.
3. Shape the meat into a loaf and place in the slow cooker. Pour the soup and sour cream mixture on top.
4. Cook on a low setting for about 10 hours before serving.

Serves 8
Per Serving
Calories	425
Fat	24 g.
Carbs	18 g.
Protein	12 g.

Holiday Treats for Any Party

Apple Crisp

One Pot Holiday Dessert

Want to make a delicious dessert for the whole family, but don't want to spend all day working on it? This one pot holiday dessert is the perfect solution.

Ingredients:
1/3 c. pecans, chopped
2/3 c. oats, quick cooking
12 ginger snaps
8 sliced and peeled apples
1 tsp. cinnamon
1 Tbsp. flour
2 Tbsp. sugar
¼ tsp. nutmeg
2 c. milk
1 pack pudding, vanilla
¼ c. melted butter

Directions:
1. Whisk the sugar and flour together in a bowl. Place the apples inside and coat them all over before putting into the slow cooker.
2. Pulse the ginger snaps in a food processor until a fine powder. Place in a bowl along with the pecans, butter, and oats. Pour this mixture on top of the apples before cooking.
3. Cook on a low setting for about 3 hours.
4. While the apples are cooking, mix the pudding with the boiling milk. Whisk until smooth then add in the nutmeg.
5. When the apples are done, pour the sauce on top of them in the slow cooker and serve warm.

Serves 12
Per Serving
Calories   266
Fat   12 g.
Carbs   13 g.

Protein   1 g.

Apple Crisp

Apple crisp on a cold day around winter is the perfect solution. It can warm up the soul and tastes so good!

Ingredients:
¼ c. almonds, sliced
12 chopped wafers
6 Tbsp. melted butter
1 c. cranberries
10 sliced and peeled apples
1 tsp. cinnamon
½ c. sugar
1 pack vanilla pudding, instant
Vanilla ice cream

Directions:
1. Take the cinnamon, fruits, ¼ cup of the sugar, the butter, and the pudding mix and mix them together.
2. Move this mixture over to the slow cooker. Cook this on a low setting for about 6 hours or until cooked through.
3. In another bow, mix together the sugar, butter, nuts, and wafers so they are well combined.
4. Place this into the microwave and let it heat up for about 90 seconds. Sprinkle over the apples and then serve with a scoop of vanilla ice cream.

Serves 8
Per Serving
Calories   278
Fat   16 g.
Carbs   22 g.
Protein   2g.

Rice Pudding

Many people remember getting to enjoy rice pudding while going out to visit grandma during the holidays. Now you can make your very own at home.

Ingredients:
1 tsp. cinnamon
1 Tbsp. sugar
1 can evaporated milk
1 can condensed milk
1 tsp. vanilla
½ c. raisins
3 c. cooked white rice

Directions:
1. Use some cooking spray in the slow cooker to avoid any sticking.
2. Next, bring out a bowl and mix together the two milks, vanilla, raisins, and white rice. Pour this into the slow cooker.
3. Place the lid on top and let this cook for 4 hours on a low setting. Stir and then add the cinnamon and sugar on top before serving.

Serves 12
Per Serving

Calories	313
Fat	12 g.
Carbs	19 g.
Protein	4 g.

Chocolate Peanut Drops

These treats are delicious and quick to make, so make a few extra batches and bring them to all of your holiday parties.

Ingredients:
3 lbs. white almond bark
1 chocolate bar
1 jar peanuts, salted
1 jar unsalted peanuts

Directions:
1. Take all of the ingredients and pour them together into the slow cooker. Place the lid on top of it all.
2. Cook this for about 2 ½ hours on a low setting. When this is done, turn off your slow cooker and allow it to cool.
3. Mix the ingredients around before dropping onto some wax paper in teaspoons. Cool down completely before serving.

Serves 12
Per Serving
Calories   299
Fat   13 g.
Carbs   5 g.
Protein   7 g.

Chocolate Cake

Need something simple and decadent to serve your guests? This chocolate cake only takes you a bit to make and can have your guests talking for hours.

Ingredients:
¼ c. chocolate chips
¼ c. water
1 Tbsp. margarine
¼ c. peanut butter
1 egg
2 ½ c. brownie mix
2 Tbsp. cocoa
¾ c. water
½ c. brown sugar

Directions:
1. Bring out a pan and bring the cocoa, sugar, and water to boil. Once these are hot, you can whisk in the rest of the ingredients.
2. Pour this into your slow cooker. Place the lid on top and let this cook on a high setting for about 2 hours.
3. Give the cake some time to cool down before serving.

Serves 10
Per Serving
Calories   215
Fat   6 g.
Carbs   23 g.
Protein   2 g.

Caramel Apples

Even though Halloween is over doesn't mean that you can't enjoy some tasty caramel apples during the holiday!

Ingredients:
¼ tsp. cinnamon
8 caramel candies, crushed
4 Tbsp. butter
12 crushed candies, red hot
8 Tbsp. brown sugar
½ c. apple juice
4 peeled and cored apples

Directions:
1. Arrange the apples inside the slow cooker. Surround with the apple juice.
2. Fill the fruits with the butter, candies, and the brown sugar. Sprinkle on some cinnamon and place the lid on top.
3. Cook this on a low setting for about 2 hours or until the apples are soft. Serve the apples warm.

Serves 4
Per Serving

Calories	199
Fat	5 g.
Carbs	18 g.
Protein	4 g.

Conclusion

Cooking for the holidays doesn't have to be stressful. While you are already busy with all of your other obligations during the holiday season, you can rest assured that your guests and family will be pleased with the delicious meals you are planning.

Just throw some of these great Christmas meals into the slow cooker on your way out the door, and you will soon have the best meals that will bring back the memories of your own childhood without all the extra work of cooking.

Thank You

Dear Readers,

Thank you so much for buying my book. I love to cook and sharing recipes with friends and family is something I have always done. From the time my own Mom gave me her recipes I have found it one of the best ways to keep relationships alive even when years and miles keep us apart.

I am always looking for ways to improve so if you enjoyed this book or have suggestions to make it better, feel free to leave a review.

Again, thank you for your readership and happy cooking!

Bree

CPSIA information can be obtained at www.ICGtesting.com
Printed in the USA
LVIW01n1444150616
492729LV00009B/42